Contents

Decisions

It is our choices ... that show what we truly are, far more than our abilities.

J.K.Rowling, *Harry Potter and the Chamber of Secrets.*

Growing up is often more about making decisions – especially the *right* decisions – than it is about growing taller or stronger. Our ability to make good decisions **defines** the sort of person we become. Our decisions reflect our thinking and can have an impact on ourselves, of course, but can also impact on our friends, family and the world around us.

Choices come in all sorts of categories: friendship, health and nutrition, when to take a risk, when to stand up for something and when to back down. The good news is that nobody ever makes the right choices all the time. In fact, many people believe that we learn best from our mistakes. Sometimes making the right choice isn't the easy **option**. Other times, we can avoid difficulty and get ahead by learning from the mistakes or choices of others.

Did you know?
It really does take a long time to grow up! Research shows that our brains – particularly our frontal lobes, where a lot of decision-making and reasoning occurs – are still maturing even into our *twenties*!

LET'S FIND OUT

- What decisions might I need to make?
- How do I respond to difficult decisions?
- Who can I turn to when I need help or advice?
- How do my decisions impact my health?
- When is it okay to say 'no'?

defines marks out the boundaries or limits of something
option a choice you make in a particular situation

Every day, we all need to make decisions. So, how do we make good choices? Who influences us? What do we do when we make poor choices?

Persuasive letter

Down with energy drinks!

Dear *Sports Monthly*,

This weekend, I'm playing in the under 12's hockey final against Albion West Bulldogs. Albion are our number-one rivals, and I've heard that they have been training extra sessions in preparation for the big match. I would do just about anything to win this game! I've heard that energy drinks are the edge that I'll need to run circles around those puppies! The latest TV advertisement for the new Metabilizor drink says it can help **hydrate** me 10 times faster than any other energy drink *and* give me long-lasting energy to burn! But with so many **controversial** arguments about energy drinks in the media, I'm not entirely sure I want to take the risk. What are your thoughts?

Yours on the goal line!
Seamus (champion goalie)

Dear Seamus,

Quite often we see celebrities and sporting heroes on TV advertising all sorts of products, including energy drinks. Marketing and media companies are very skilful at making these items look attractive, using cool jingles and fun logos. But here are the facts: research shows that energy drinks don't always do what they claim. They will not give you 'long-lasting energy' or hydrate you any quicker than a glass of ordinary tap water. However, a standard energy drink will give you about 80 milligrams of caffeine. That's approximately equivalent to a cup of coffee – which is fine in moderation.

hydrate drink enough water to stay healthy
controversial a topic people have strong opinions about

The real problem is that energy drinks can have up to 13 teaspoons of sugar! And that's just in one can! So imagine what happens to growing bodies when they are having two, three or even four energy drinks per day? That's a lot of sugar and caffeine! It's no wonder that **over-consumption** has triggered heart attacks and **palpitations** in some teenagers.

In a recent experiment, researchers drank a variety of energy drinks and had their blood tests analysed. Their blood literally became sticky. The findings confirmed that energy drinks could lead to serious heart attacks – and even strokes!

My advice is to always read the nutrition labels on food and drink containers. If a label is full of weird-sounding ingredients, stay away! Nothing gives you energy like the right training and being 'in the zone'. Good luck in the finals – and drink lots of water!

over-consumption eating or drinking too much
palpitations irregular heartbeats

Breakaway tasks

Remembering

1 About how many teaspoons of sugar are there in one energy drink?

2 What happened to the researchers' blood after they drank energy drinks?

Understanding

3 List the reasons for and against consuming energy drinks.

4 Create a Venn diagram showing the similarities and differences between water and energy drinks. If possible, compare the nutrition labels on an energy drink and a bottle of water.

Applying

5 Write a list of energy drinks. Conduct a survey of your class and tally the popularity of the different brands. Discuss the marketing of each brand. How do they attract the buyer? What age group are they aimed at? Are they aimed at boys or girls?

6 Use the Internet to investigate which foods have the same quantity of sugar as an average energy drink. Discuss your findings with the class. Were there any surprises?

Analysing

7 What are the myths and facts about energy drinks that may have lead to Seamus' misconceptions? Create and complete a T-chart headed 'Fact' and 'Opinion' using facts from the text.

Evaluating

8 Use the Internet to create a mind map exploring the dangers of excessive sugar consumption in students of your age.

9 Write a letter to the editor of a local paper explaining why energy drinks should be advertised differently.

Creating

10 Create an advertisement for a new brand of exciting energy drink called 'H_2O' (better known as water!). Explain why water is so much better for you than energy drinks.

Choices

Today my class started Health Education with Ms Klein, and we knew it was going to be *sooo* embarrassing! Jenny Tranh said that any break from maths – especially *fractions* – was a good thing, but personally, I felt more comfortable with numerators and denominators!

"Decisions, decisions!" said Ms Klein with an air of confidence, as she spun around and started walking around the class circle. Okay, I thought: so far, so good!

"What was the last big decision you had to make …" Ms Klein stopped speaking and waved her finger around the room until she came to "… Alec?"

Alec looked startled. "Um … what to have for breakfast?" He shrugged. That made everybody giggle.

"Okay, that's a reasonably good answer, Alec. What made it a big decision? Was it life-changing?"

Alec pretended to think hard about it, screwing his face up in concentration. "Yeah, pretty big. But probably not life-changing," he said, grinning.

"Well, I suppose it can be seen as a big decision – especially if we love our breakfast. It is the most important meal of the day!" Ms Klein smiled.

It was obviously time to **delve** deeper, as this was when Ms Klein started targeting us with some very interesting questions. She also switched the word *decisions* for *choices*.

"What are some important choices that we need to make in life?" asked Ms Klein. Hands went up.

---

delve find out more information

"Good health choices," said Edwina.

"Friendship choices," said Petra.

"Doing the right thing," said Rowan.

"Such as … ?" asked Ms Klein.

"Treating people with respect," said Francesco.

"Looking after family and friends," said Daiki.

"Saying no," said Nina.

At that point there were a few confused faces in the class. Ms Klein asked for **clarification**. "When can saying 'no' be making the right choice?"

Nina spoke up. "Saying no to things like alcohol and drugs can help keep us safe and healthy."

"Exactly," said Ms Klein. "Sometimes people are faced with making big decisions about whether or not to smoke, drink alcohol or take illegal drugs. So why do you think people make poor choices about their health, especially when they know something is bad for them, such as smoking?"

"They're curious," said Mick.

"Because they think it'll make them feel good," said Stella.

"Yes, sometimes," said Ms Klein.

"**Peer pressure**," said Akash. "Because it can be hard to say no."

"Ah! Precisely," said Ms Klein. "People of your age – eleven, twelve and above – are actually the highest-risk age group for **experimentation** or trying new things. And I mean alcohol and smoking, as well as other forms of risk-taking. Peer pressure is a huge part of that. It's **disheartening** when kids feel that that they need to take such risks in order to fit in with friends."

Ms Klein turned towards me. "Meaghan!" she said. "What would *you* do if you were at a party and a friend offered you a cigarette?"

clarification make something easier to understand
peer pressure feeling you have to do what your friends do
experimentation trying something to find out what it is like
disheartening making you lose hope

But before I could respond, Ms Klein said, "Hang on. Let's role-play a possible scenario. Alec, stand up and offer Meaghan a cigarette."

"Whoa!" said Alec, putting his hands up innocently. As my cheeks began to redden, the class gave a laugh.

"Now Alec," said Ms Klein, "I'm not accusing you! Sometimes thinking through scenarios like this can help you organise your thoughts. So, Meaghan, what would you do?"

"I – I would say no," I stammered. I could feel my face glowing brighter as I stared at the whole class. I couldn't look at Alec!

"Really? Would it be *that* easy?" asked Ms Klein. She turned and asked the question again to the class. I could see everybody thinking. It actually got me thinking, too!

"You've got thirty seconds to discuss what you *would* say, remembering that 90 per cent of adult smokers actually started when they were kids."

Alec and I actually had a good conversation about it! We decided that being positive and not negative was the way to go. In fact it was *so* good, Ms Klein asked us to role-play in front of the whole class! The first time I ran out of excuses to say 'no'.

Then Ms Klein handed me a fact file.

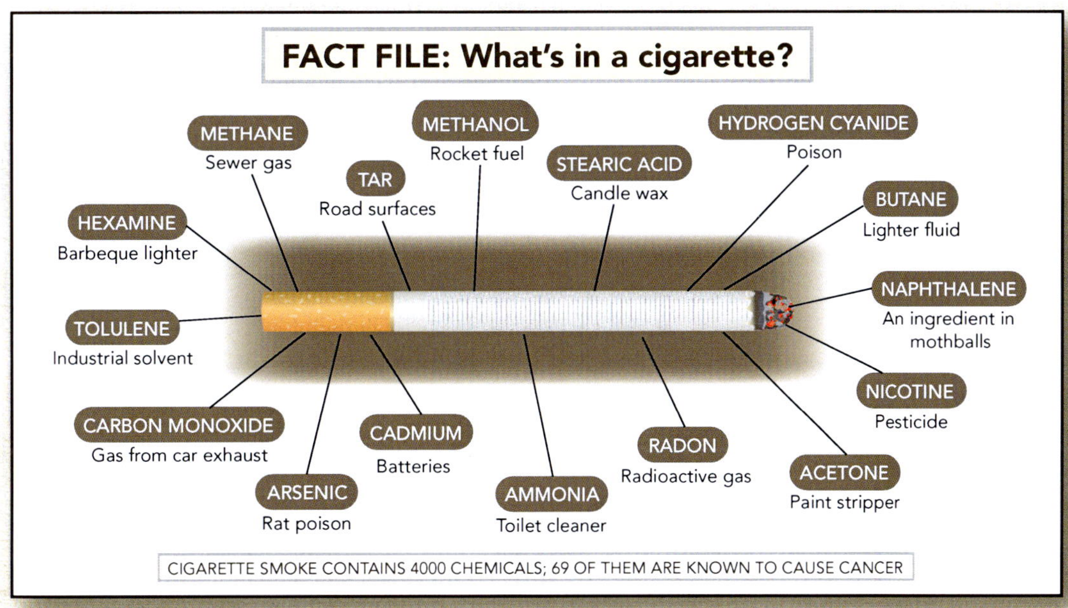

I stared at it in amazement. It was headed, 'What's in a cigarette?' "Now let's see what happens when Meaghan has a bit of knowledge about cigarettes," Ms Klein said to the class.

"Here, try this," said Alec, as he handed me an imaginary cigarette.

I took it and stared at it as if it was real.

"Want a light?" Alec pretended to hold a lighter out for me.

"No. No, thanks. I like being a non-smoker," I said. "I want to play netball for Australia, and I need to keep fit and healthy."

"Come on, it's just *one*!" he persisted.

I glanced at the card "You know, Alec, smoking is highly addictive," I said. He shrugged.

"In fact, cigarette smoke contains more than 4000 chemicals," I said. Alec blinked. "Including some that are used to make pesticides, batteries, fuel and toilet cleaners," I said. Alec looked startled.

"Not to mention carbon monoxide, which is the poisonous fume that comes out from car exhausts," I went on.

I looked around and could see a sea of very shocked faces. Alec hadn't been expecting that!

"Come on, everybody's having one," he said.

I dropped the card by my side. "And I haven't even got to the part about tar actually forming inside your lungs or cancer, or —"

Alec put his hands up in defeat. "OK, I quit!" He smiled.

I can't believe I had actually beaten him! And, with everyone clapping my decision, I felt really … *powerful*!

I wonder if I will be brave enough to stand up and make good choices when the time comes. I guess the key will be having the knowledge and confidence to make the right choice … and knowing that good friends support you no matter what!

Breakaway tasks

Remembering

1 What excuses does Meaghan use to refuse the cigarette from Alec?

2 How many ingredients from cigarettes can you remember? Draw a diagram of a cigarette and label the ingredients.

Understanding

3 In a small group, discuss the pressures that students of your age experience about smoking and similar issues. List ways to address these issues.

4 What strategies does Meaghan use in order to stand up to Alec? What else could Meaghan have done in this situation?

Applying

5 How do you think you would approach a situation like Meaghan's, when Alec tries to talk her into smoking? Write a section of dialogue that realistically portrays what might happen.

6 What are some useful strategies for learning to say 'no'? Brainstorm a list of possible strategies to use in different scenarios. What strategies work best? Why?

Analysing

7 Create a mind-map exploring the subject of risk-taking. Can taking risks be a healthy thing? Or should we avoid all risks?

8 What makes a decision a *bad* one? Choose one decision from the text and write it at the centre of a mind-map. Analyse the range of possible outcomes, including possible consequences, and add them to your mind-map.

Evaluating

9 Meaghan has a long list of reasons not to share a cigarette with Alec. In your opinion, which reason works best, and why? Write a paragraph justifying your choice.

Creating

10 Design a slogan for a help line or a website aimed at helping students of your age make decisions and say 'no' to peer pressure.

Cyber safety

If you think 'cyber safety' is about being safe online, you are absolutely correct! But what does it really mean? Unlike water safety, cyber safety is less about being physically safe and more about protecting yourself from bullies and people you don't know, and knowing steps to take when you don't feel safe. As more **social networks** become available, the need to be 'cyber smart' is becoming more important.

Let's have a look at the latest cyber-safety advice for kids aged 8 to 12.

Mobile phones

These days mobile phones are used not only to make calls, but also to play **interactive** games, for banking and to search websites.

It is important to:

- use your phone to contact people you know and trust
- keep your **Bluetooth** set to 'hidden'
- watch out for scams
- set your privacy settings
- call your provider asap if you lose your phone.

Don't:

- send images or personal details to people you don't know
- respond to negative, threatening messages or behaviour
- forward or send anything you wouldn't be comfortable sending to a parent.

Online games

With interactive games now collecting more and more personal information, remember to:

- use a nickname online
- block unfriendly players from your players list.

Don't:

- give out any personal information
- play games that may be unsuitable
- enter chat rooms or forums based on your game unsupervised.

Remember, if someone is displaying bullying behaviour online, it's a problem! You can:

- tell someone
- not reply
- block them, even if you need a parent or teacher to help
- report them: games and social media have ways of doing this
- call Kids' Helpline on 1800 55 1800.

Importantly, if you know someone is being targeted in an unsafe way – speak up! Don't circulate stories or images. Get help from someone you trust.
See the Australian Communication and Media Authority (ACMA) website for more information and tips for cyber safety.

social networks websites or apps where users post comments, messages and photos

interactive a computer program or TV system that allows you to communicate directly with it

Bluetooth method of connecting phones, computers and other devices

Breakaway tasks

Remembering

1 What does it mean to be cyber safe?

2 What two things can you do if you are being bullied online?

Understanding

3 Choose one of the categories 'Online Games' or 'Mobile Phones' and copy the key points/advice. Next to each safety tip, provide a reason *why* the advice is important for your safety.

4 Write a persuasive paragraph convincing your classmates to follow proper safety steps while online.

Applying

5 Create a three-column table of your current online routines and behaviours. In the left column, list the device or programs you use. In the middle column, record your current safety measures. In the final column, write tips from the text to improve your online safety.

6 Draw a 'looks like, sounds like, feels like' chart about cyber safety. Add suitable images and text.

Analysing

7 Which three tips from the text are the easiest for you to adopt? Discuss your responses with a partner, then share with the class.

Evaluating

8 Rank the tips from the text from most important to least important. Discuss your findings with a classmate.

Creating

9 Create a brochure of online do's and don'ts. Add two further tips to each area.

10 Create a video advertisement, role-playing a scenario where one of your classmates uses one or more cyber safety tips. Compile these clips for class display and vote on the best three group efforts.

The Long Walk and 'Dreamtime at the G'

Interview with Michael Long

Former Essendon footballer Michael Long changed history, not just for his amazing abilities as one of the AFL greats – Long was equal fourth in the 1995 Brownlow Medal Count – but for his passionate and courageous stands against racism in football as an **Indigenous** player. He also had a massive impact after he retired.

In 2004, Long decided to walk over 650 kilometres from Melbourne to Canberra to talk with Prime Minister John Howard about the plight of Indigenous Australians. Long had a huge impact on how Indigenous Australians were being viewed.

His walk, 'the Long Walk', became an integral part of the 'Dreamtime at the G' AFL match between Essendon and Richmond, and is now a part of the AFL's Indigenous Round of football.

The following is an excerpt from the ABC News radio interview with Michael Long about the Long Walk.

"The Long Walk started in 2004 for us. It was really about, you know, where was the love for Aboriginal people? Being a footballer for the Essendon Football Club, there needed to be something deeper done …

"When we talk about reconciliation, football has done that, and obviously we're in our eighth year of 'The Long Walk', and you can see the momentum of some of the great work that's been done by football – and all football clubs for that matter – the amount of Indigenous players who have played: we're looking at Indigenous leadership … We had between twelve and fifteen thousand who walked to the MCG with us.

"Can I just say to football supporters and the Australian people … I'm just so thankful for their support and the great change that football and our Australian public have made … I just want to thank them so much."

Indigenous people or things that have always been where they are; native

Breakaway tasks

Remembering

1 Which Australian city did Michael Long walk to in order to speak with Prime Minister John Howard about the plight of Indigenous Australians?

2 How far did Michael walk, and where did he begin?

Understanding

3 Create a mind-map of the possible issues the Long Walk has addressed.

4 When you read Michael's interview, what adjectives would you use to describe the 'tone' of his speech?

Applying

5 Create a map showing the route Michael took from Melbourne to Canberra, and plot where he stopped and how long the walk took. Illustrate the map with images of Michael on the walk.

Analysing

6 Use the Internet to research and write a short biography of Michael Long, including the events that helped shape his courageous stance against racism both while he was a footballer and after his football career.

7 Read the interview section of the text again and write a brief summary. What is the main point of Michael's speech?

Evaluating

8 How do you think football has played a part in 'reconciliation' with Indigenous people?

9 From the interview section of the text, what decision or decisions did Michael Long make? Why did he feel the need to make them? What was the outcome?

Creating

10 Design a football guernsey that represents the main message outlined in Michael Long's speech.

Strands in action

Core tasks

1 Design a website about the importance of decisions. Create a homepage and three pages dealing with the topics of health, safety and wellbeing. Try using a combination of text types, such as information, persuasive and explanation.

2 Using available ICT, record a talkback radio segment where a number of callers phone in to voice their concerns over some 'big decisions'. As the host, your job is to provide support to enable your callers to make thoughtful decisions. Prepare a script before you record your show. Include the concerns of at least three different callers.

Extra tasks

1 Begin a journal recording the daily decisions you make. Record the big decisions you have to make over a week. Discuss what made the decisions 'big'? Compare these with your classmates' decisions.

2 Write a story about growing up. Use the title, 'My decisions have made me who I am today', as a prompt.

3 Write a letter to the editor of a fictitious school newspaper, persuading your readers not to give in to peer pressure. Provide a few simple strategies to help your audience!

4 Create a personal plan in which you make decisions about your lifestyle to improve your health, safety or other areas of your life. List your current behaviours and areas for improvement. Next decide *how* you could take action. Include some goals, but remember to make them SMART: Specific, Measureable, Achievable, Realistic and Timely.

Bullet points are those handy dots – or sometimes letters or numbers – that follow a colon. They:

- draw attention to important points
- identify key facts and issues
- visually break up a text
- tend to be about the same length.

Try not to overuse bullet points. Remember: they do have their uses, but not in all text types.